Coloring Dragons

by
Nina Bolen

Artwork by Nina Bolen
Layout and Design by Brian Bolen

Find more artwork by Nina Bolen by visiting online at http://www.ninabolenart.com
Follow Nina on Facebook at https://www.facebook.com/NinaBolenArt

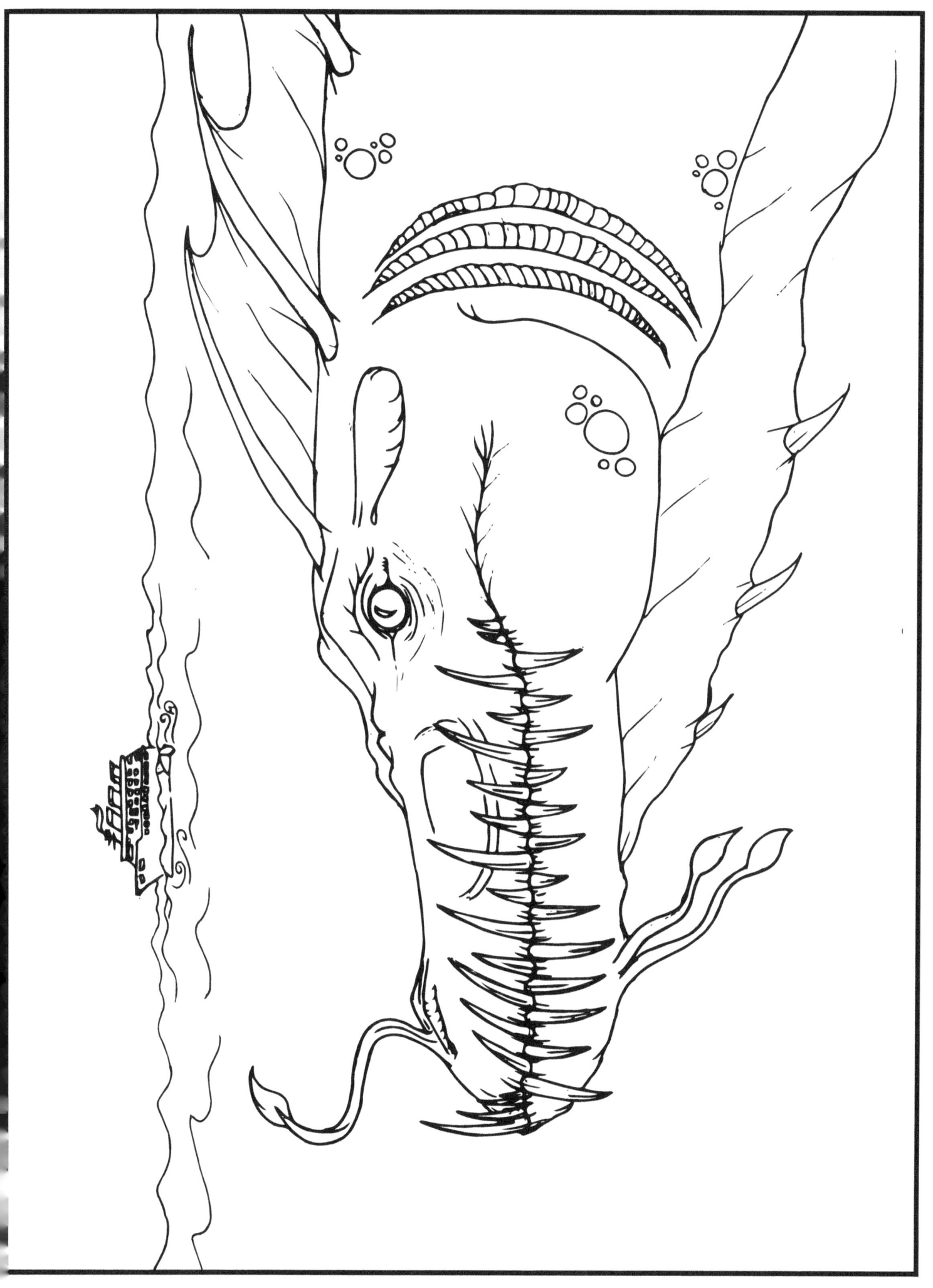

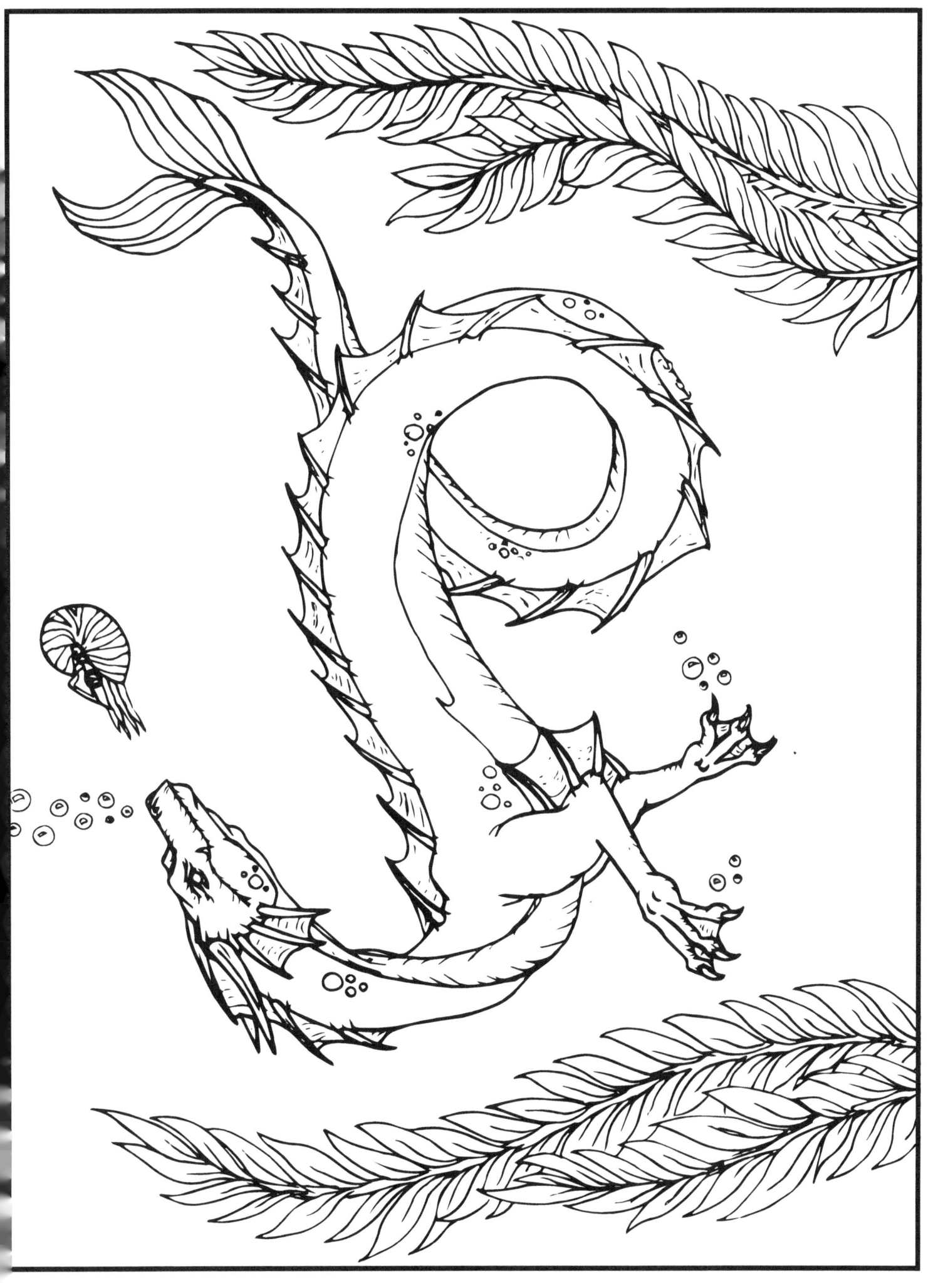

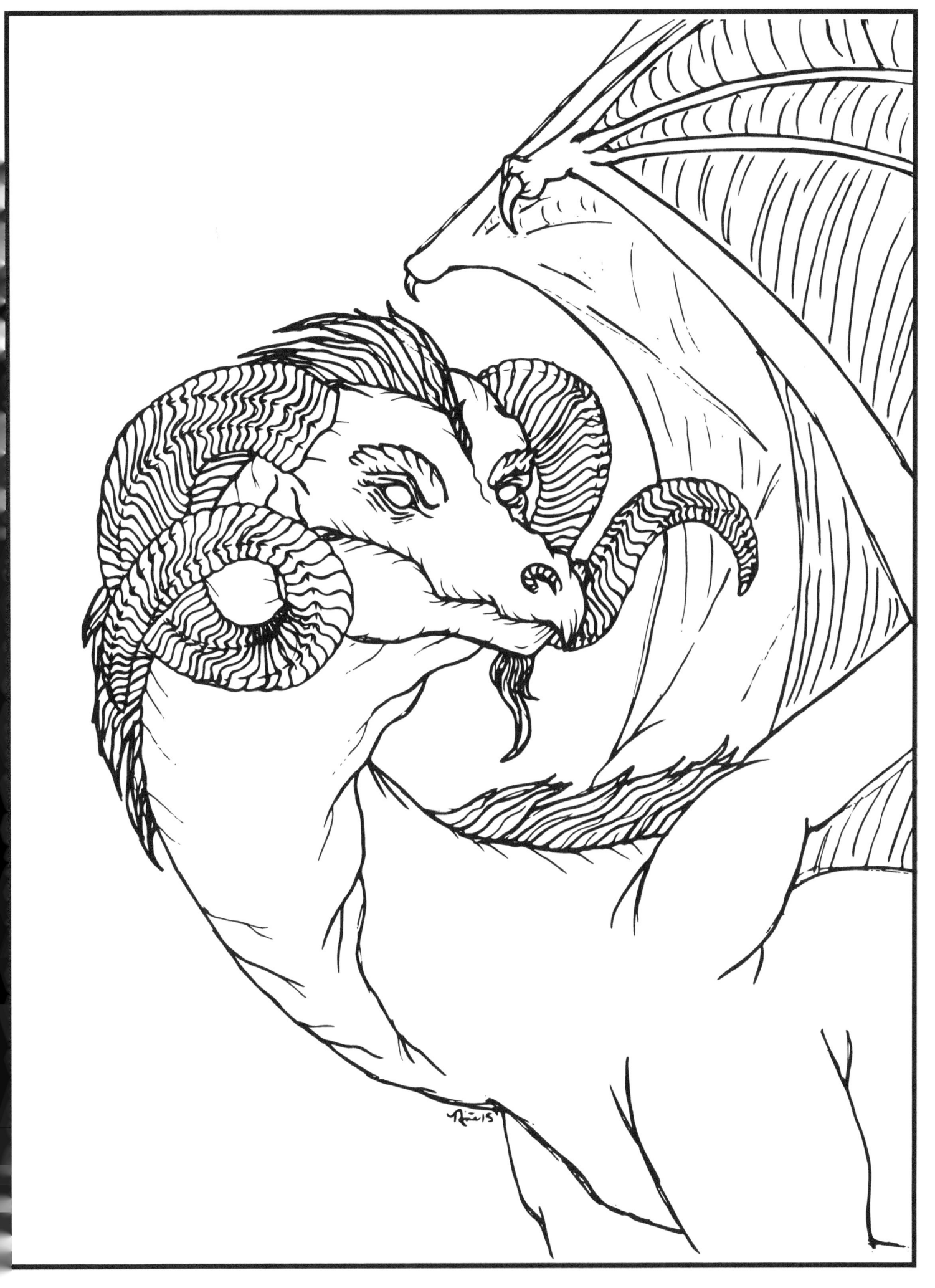

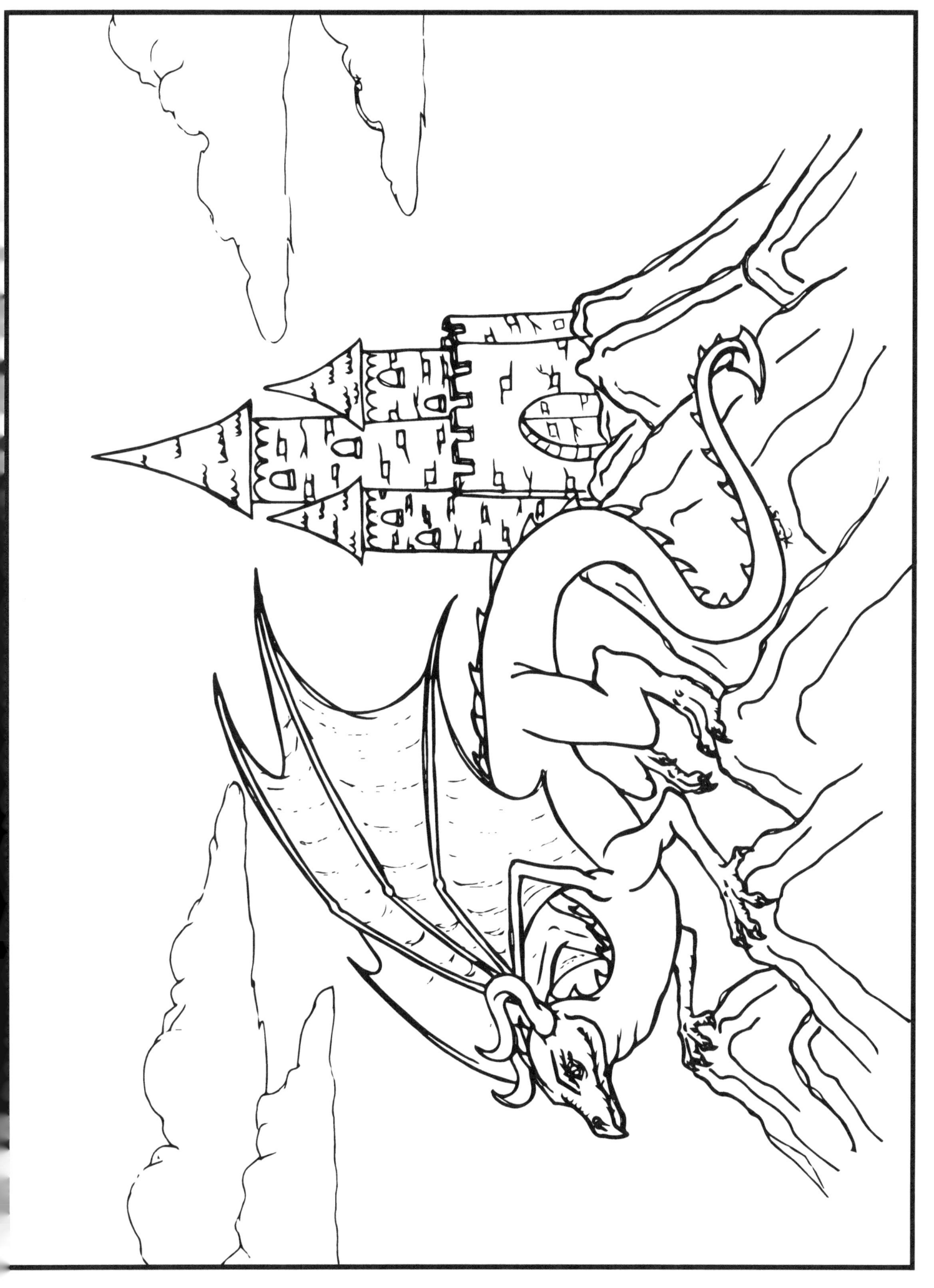

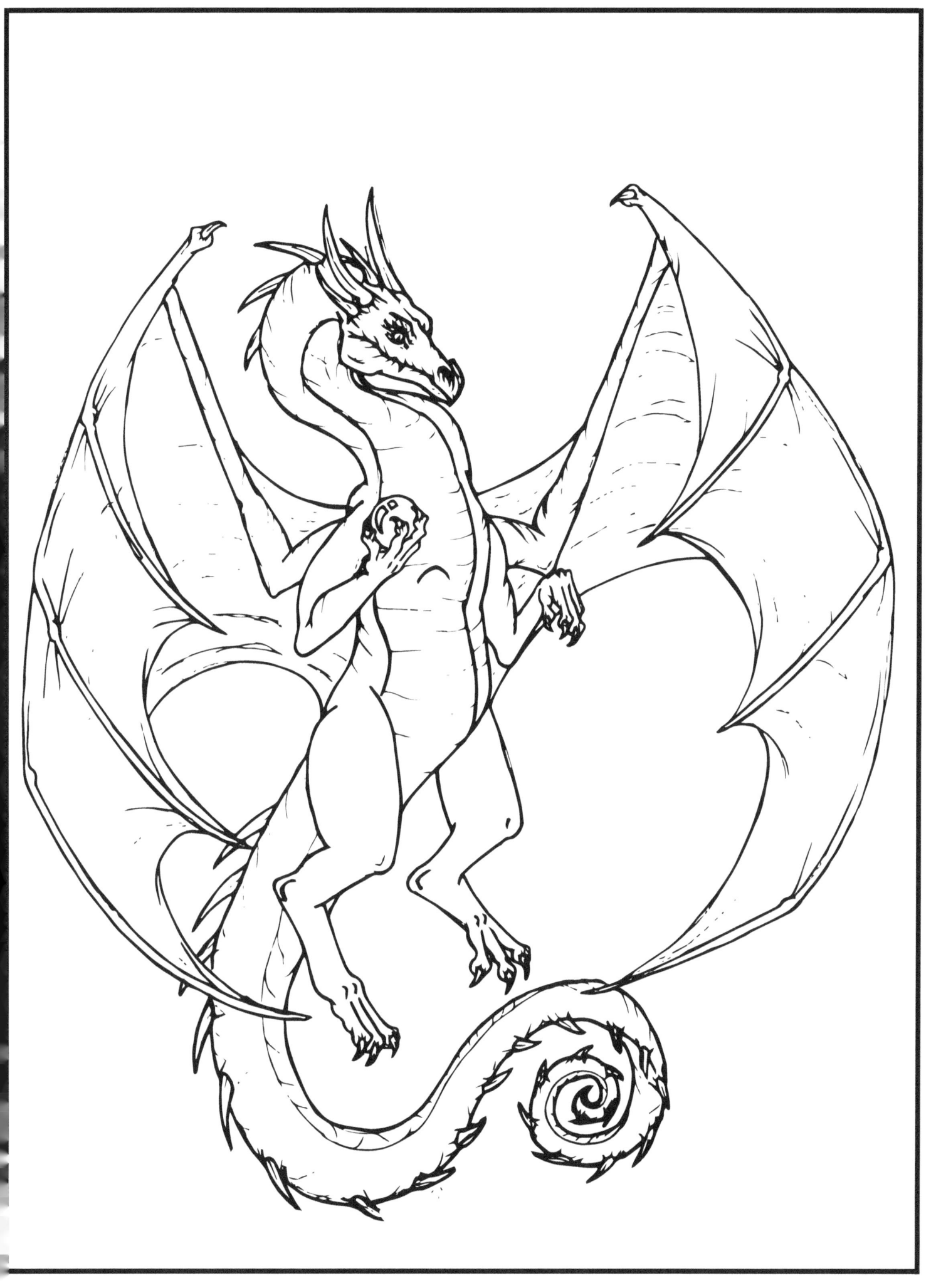

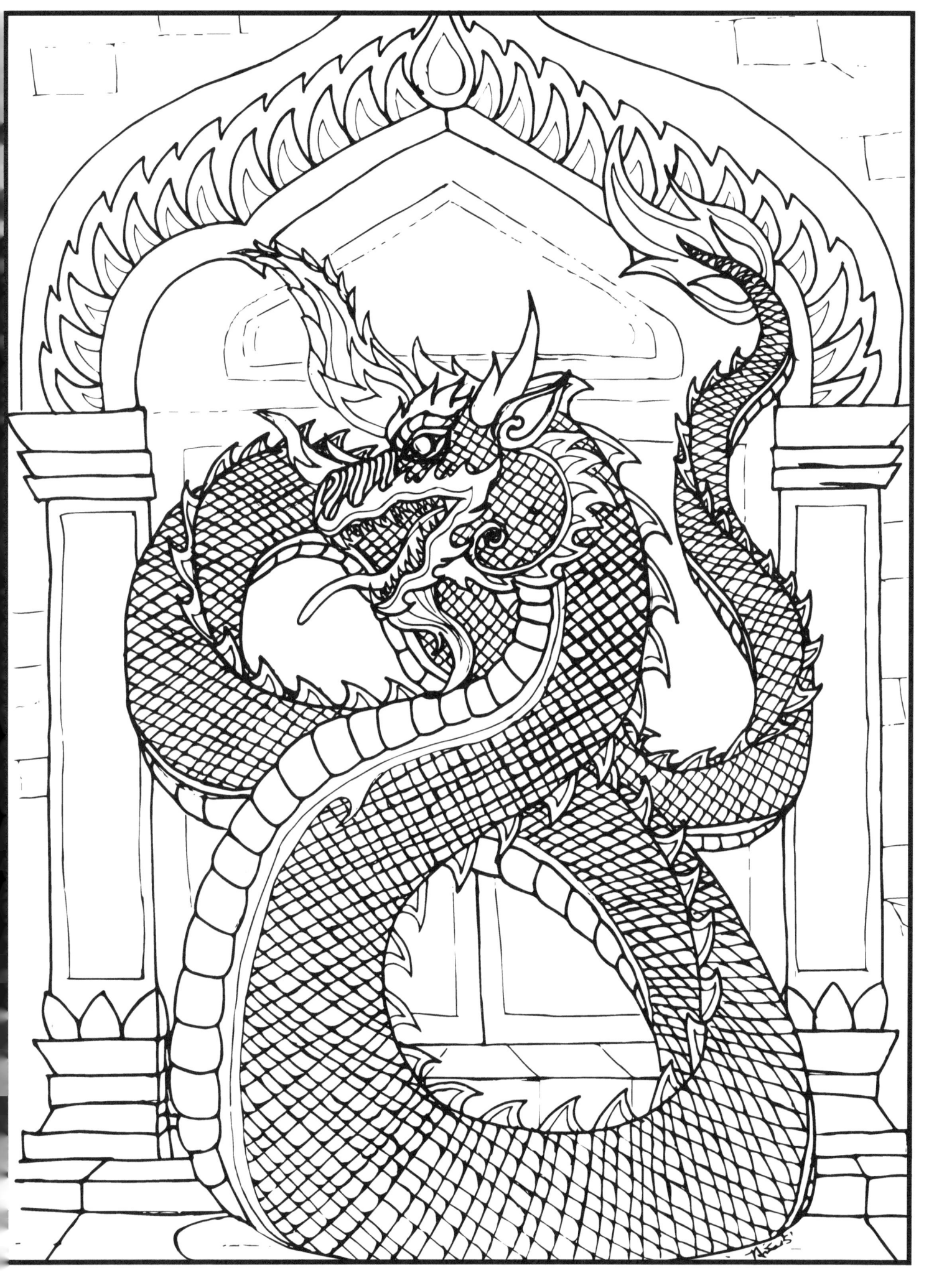

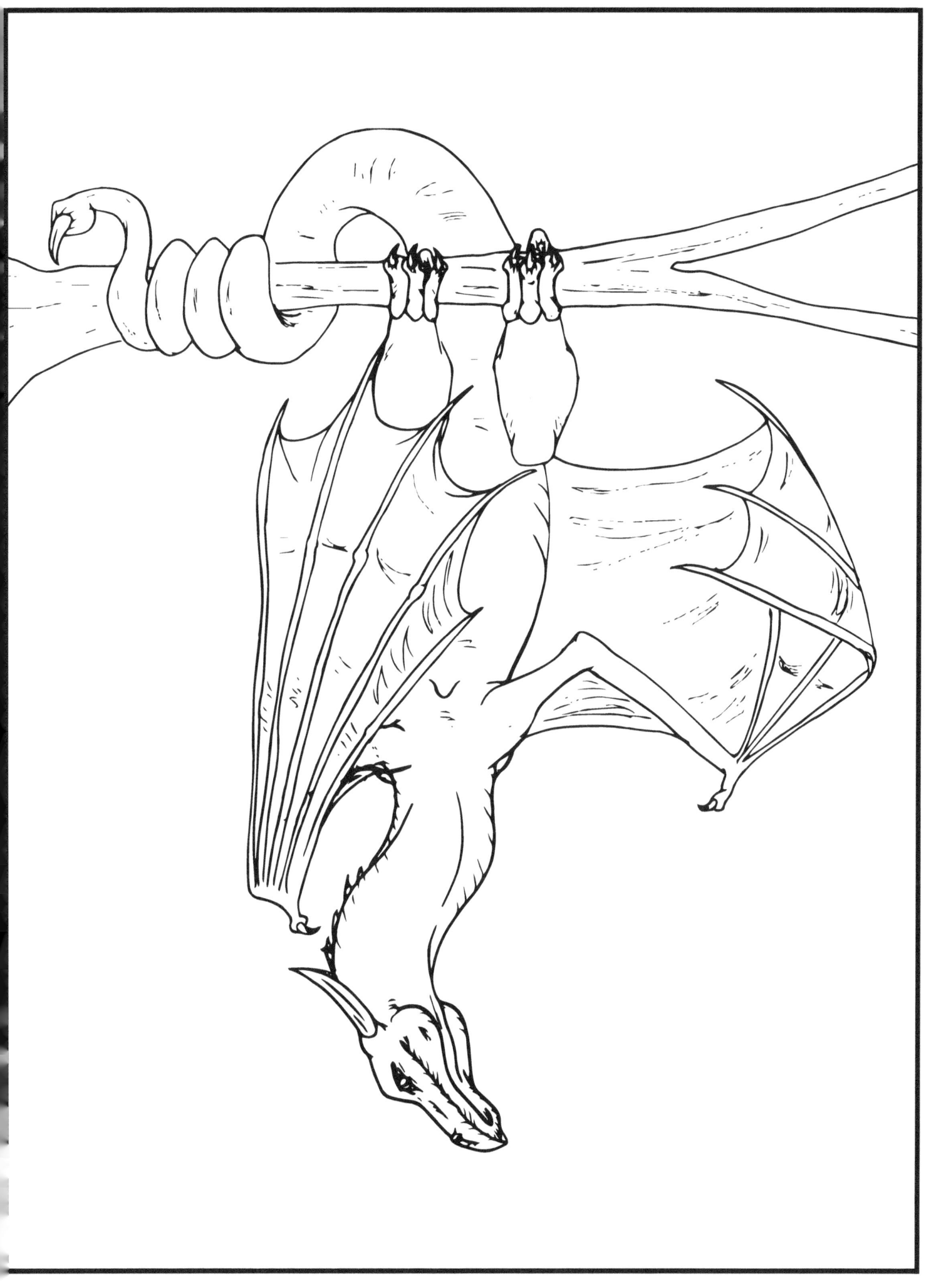

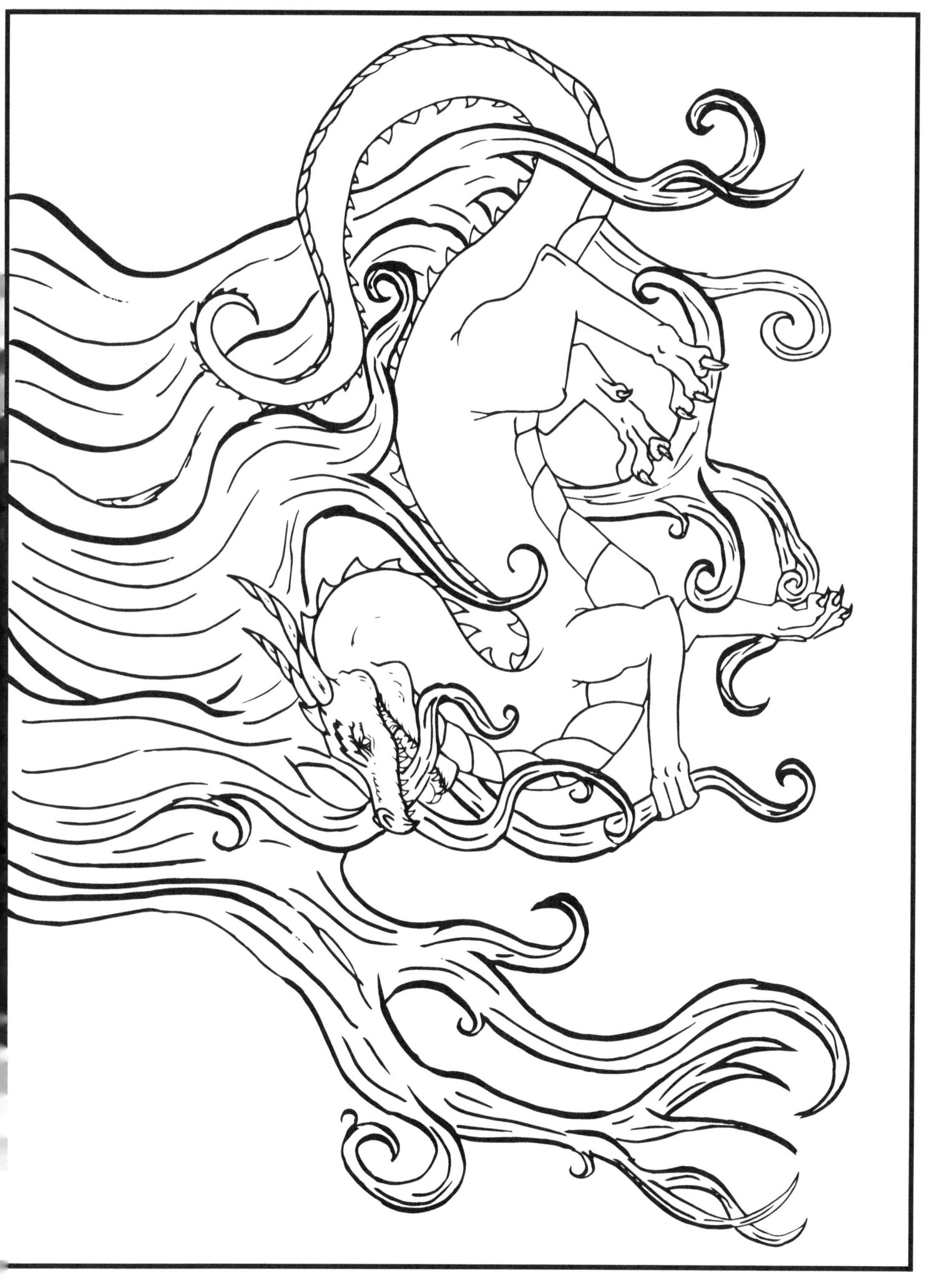

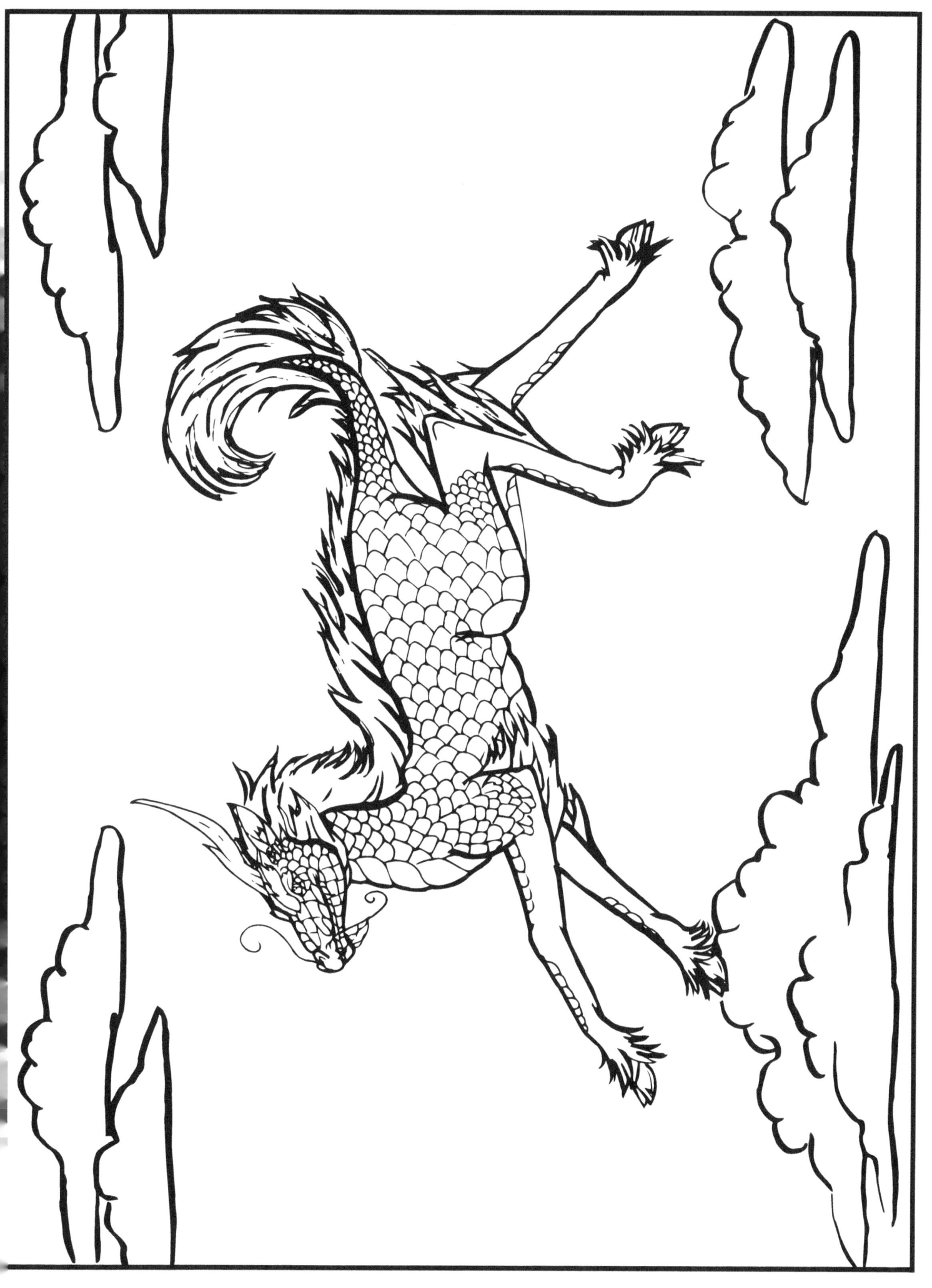

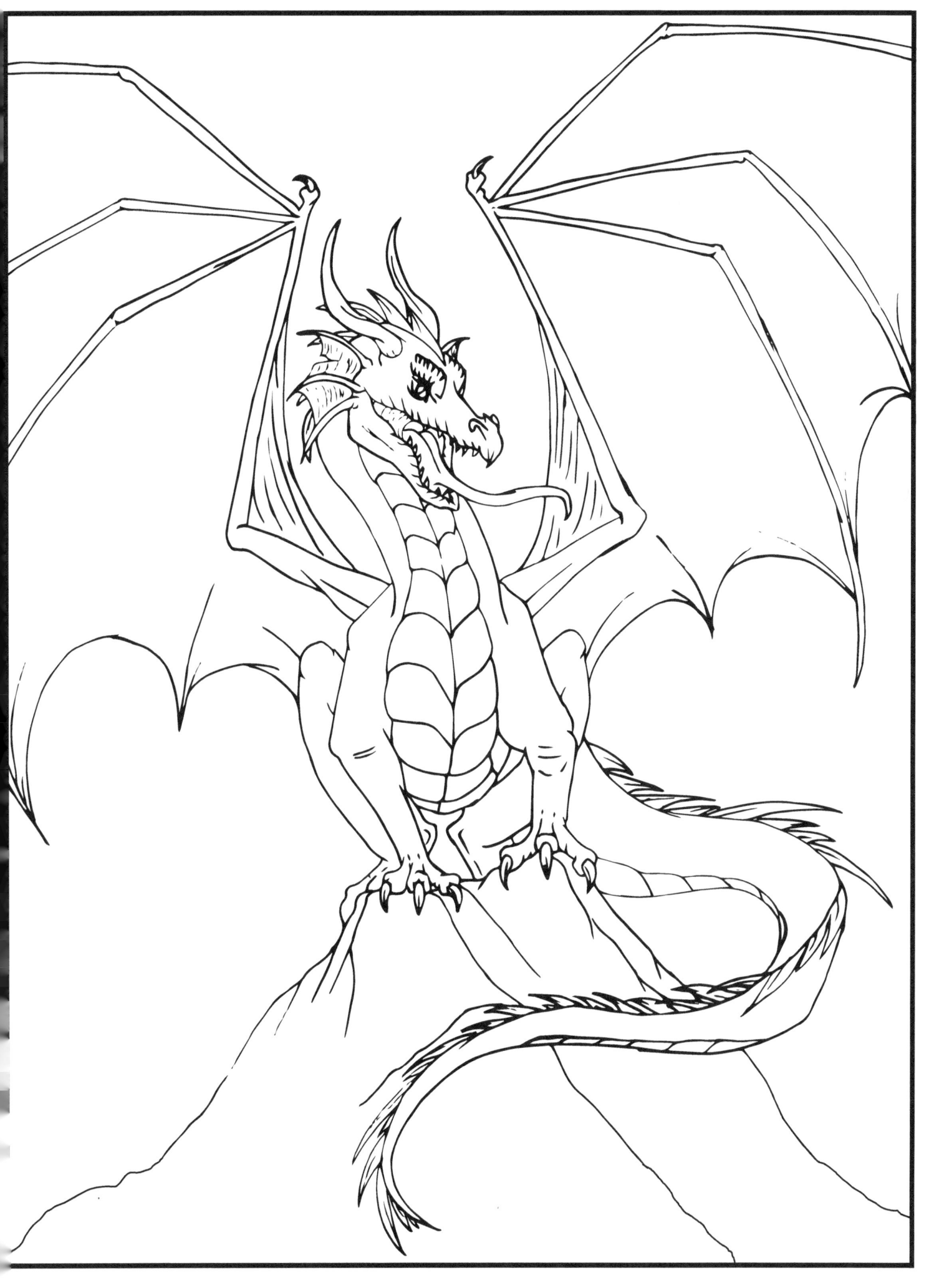

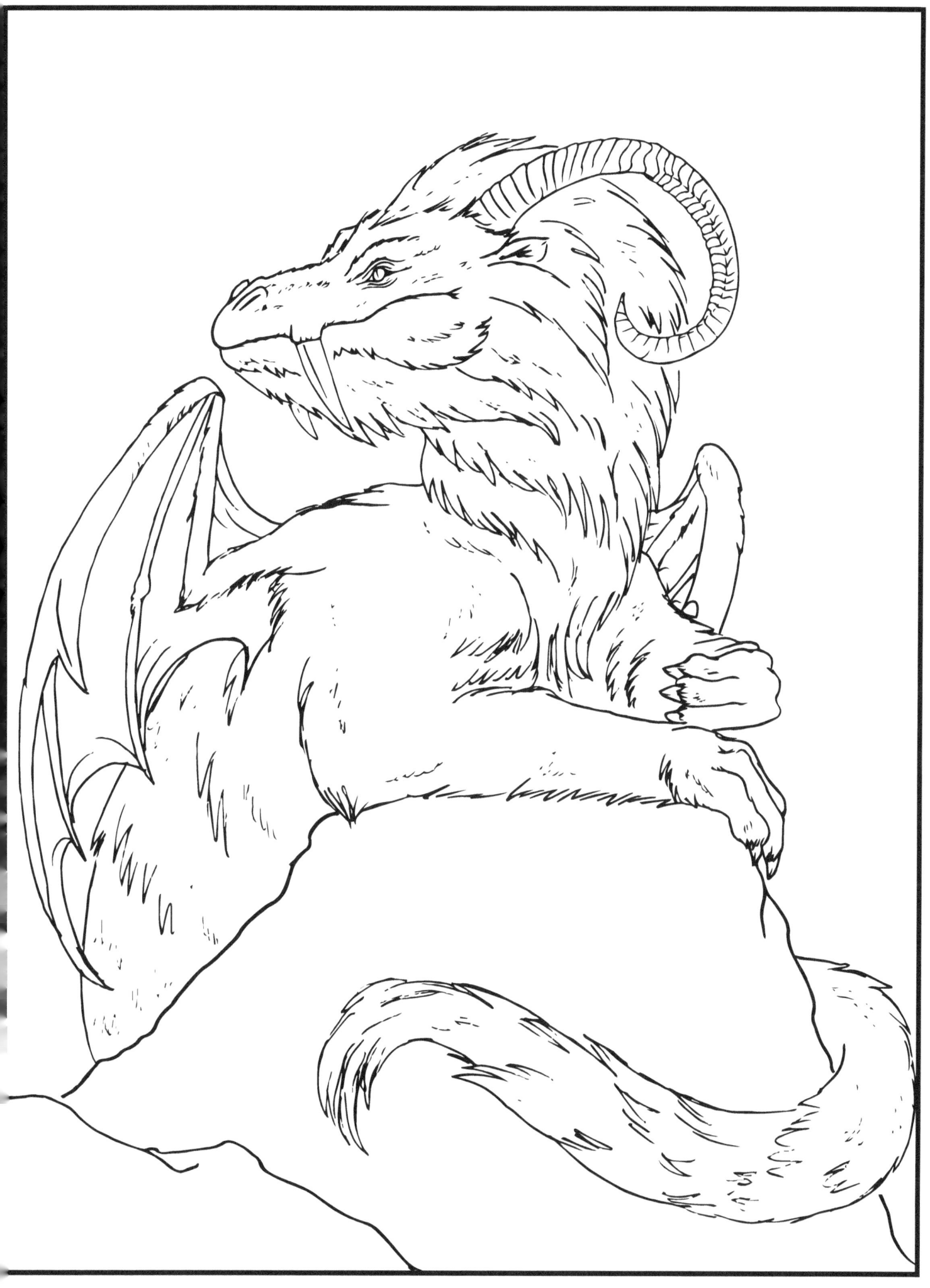

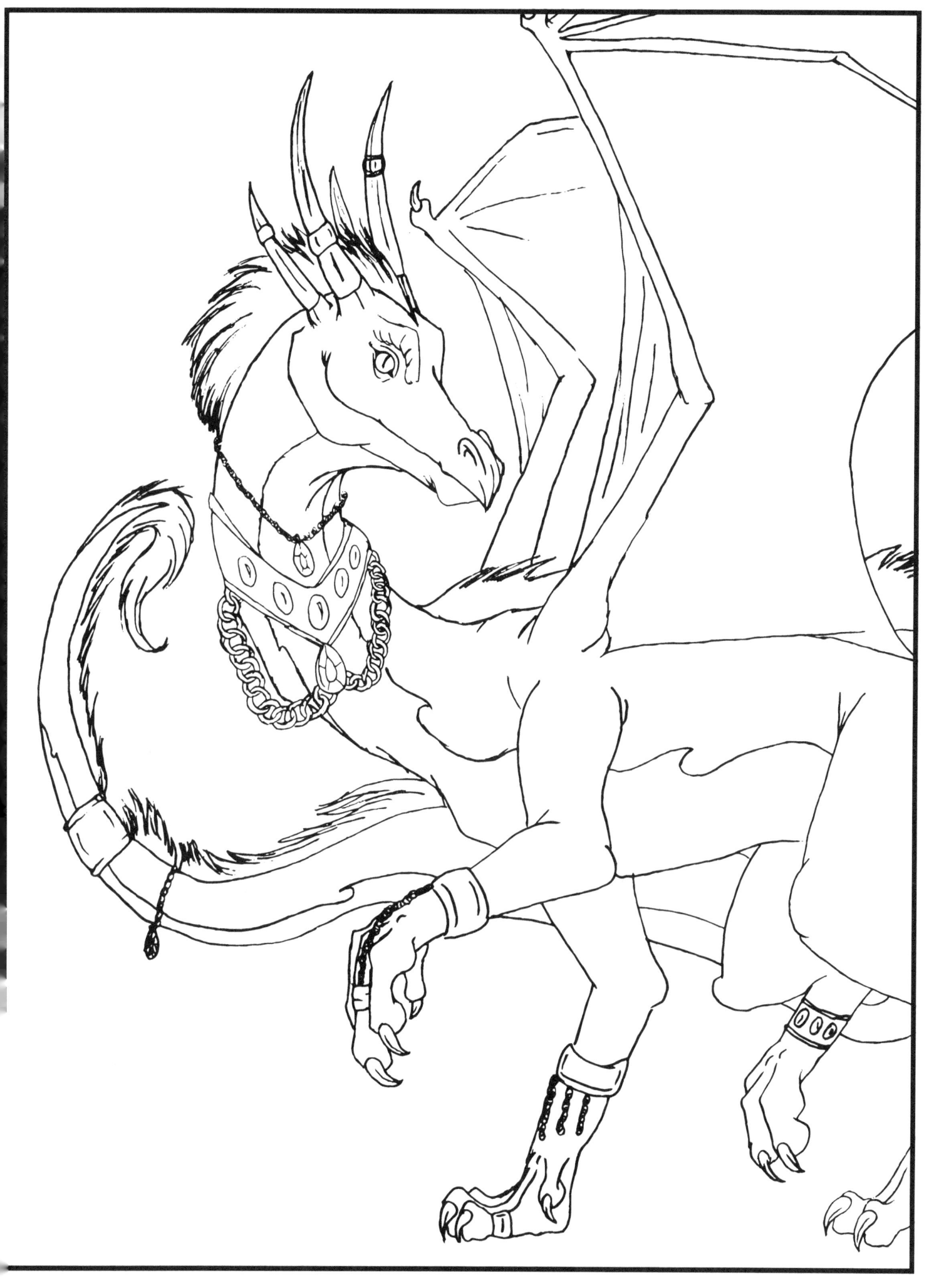

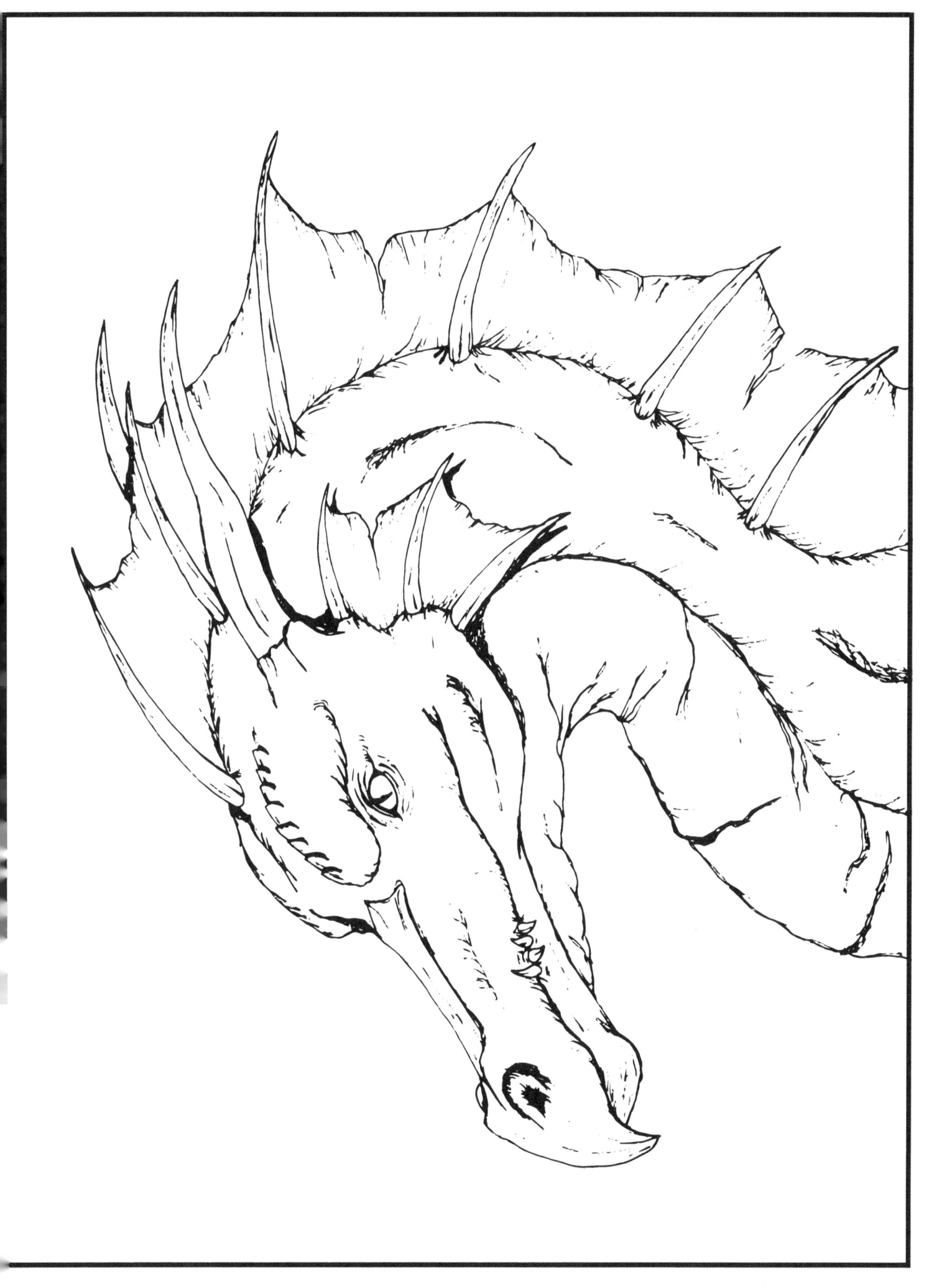

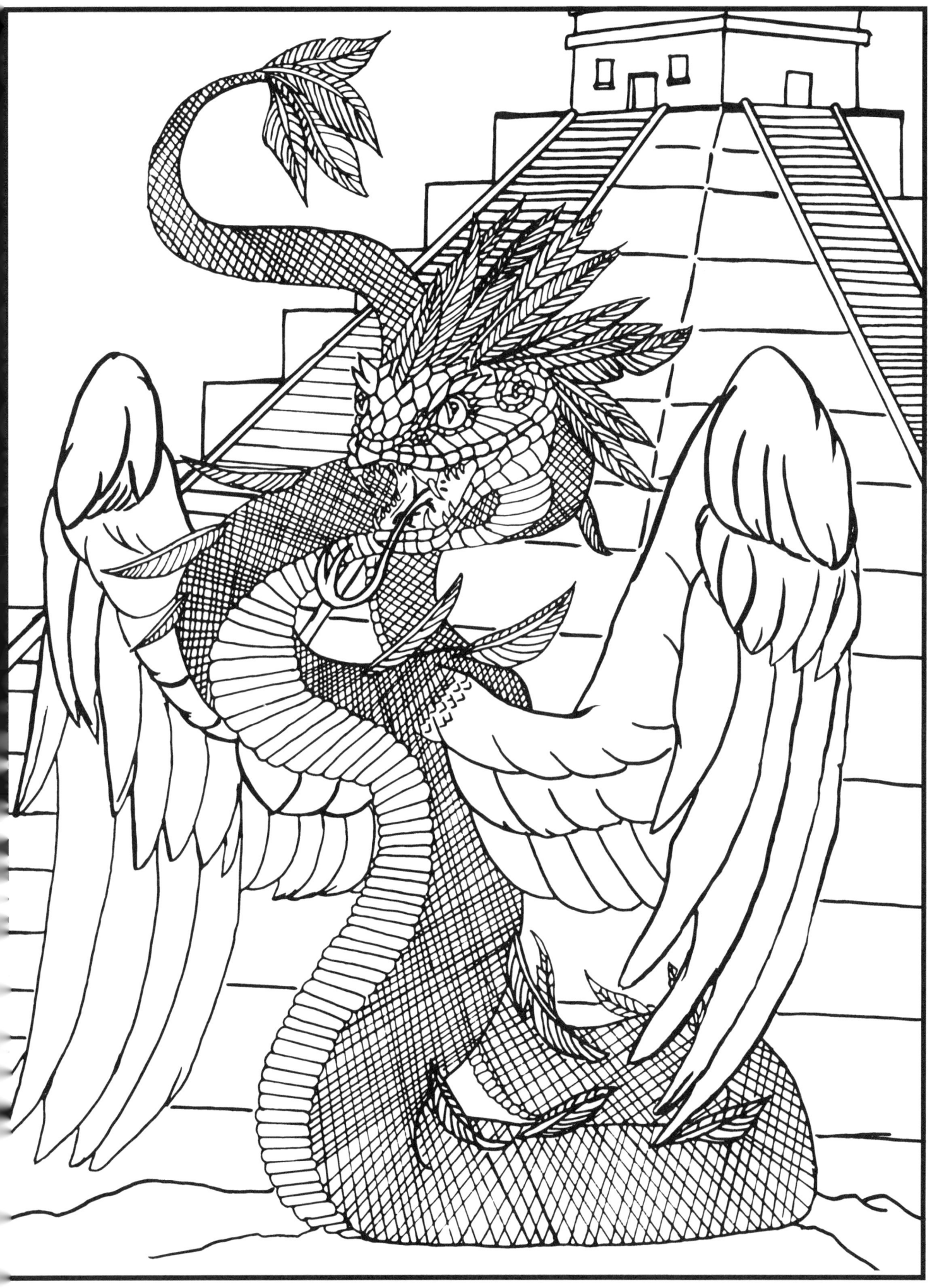

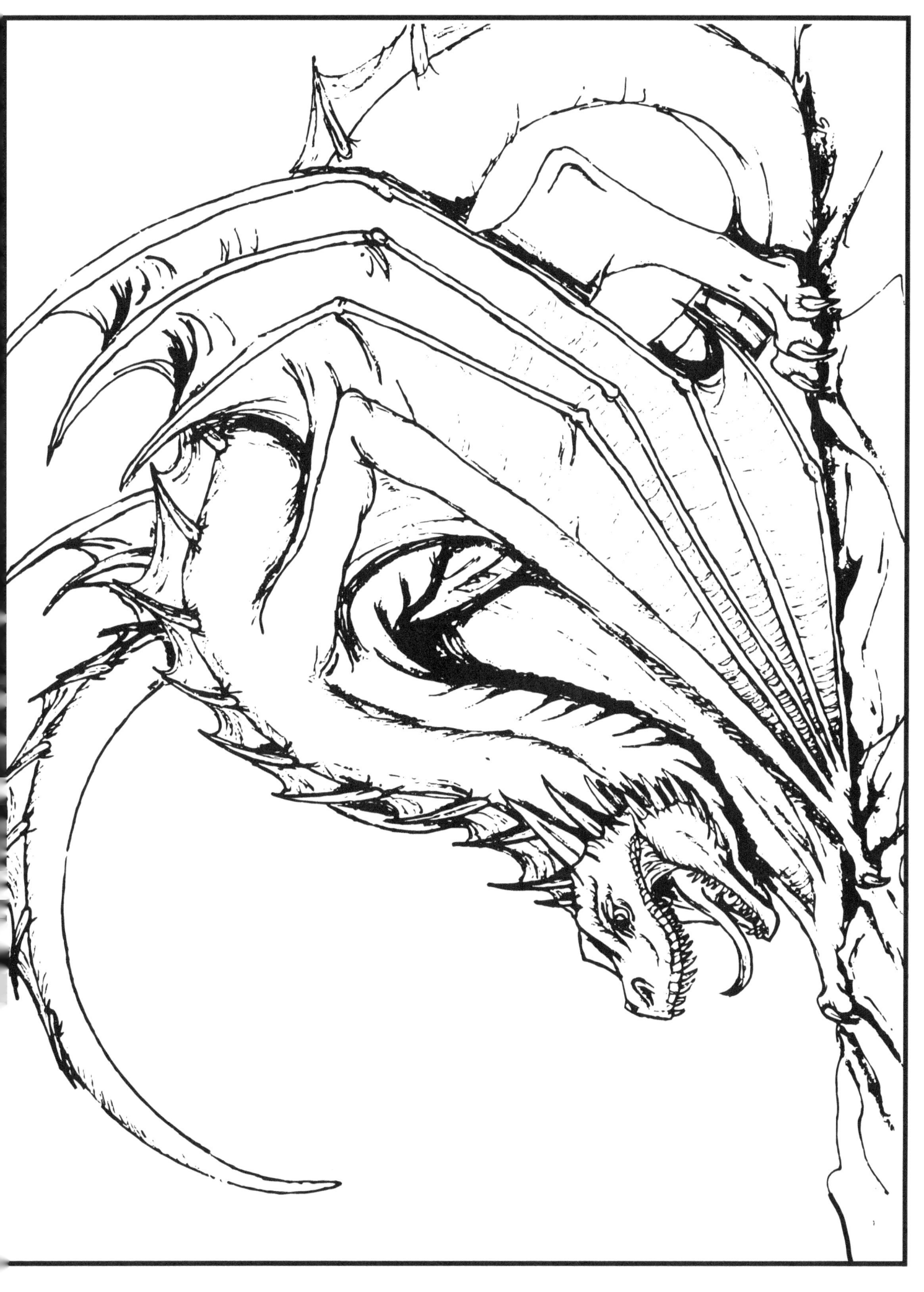